ONE ACT OF COURAGE

THE STORY OF ROSA PARKS FOR KIDS

SARAH MICHAELS

BOOKSTEM

Copyright © 2025 by Sarah Michaels

All rights reserved.

No part of this book may be reproduced in any form or by any electronic or mechanical means, including information storage and retrieval systems, without written permission from the author, except for the use of brief quotations in a book review.

CONTENTS

Introduction   5

1. GROWING UP IN THE SOUTH   11
   Life in the segregated South   14
   Learning about discrimination from an early age   17
   Rosa's love for education   21

2. LIFE UNDER SEGREGATION   25
   Different rules for Black and white people   28
   The unfairness of public transportation   31
   The Montgomery bus system   35

3. THE DAY THAT CHANGED HISTORY   39
   Arrest and consequences   42
   How Rosa's actions sparked a movement   45

4. THE MONTGOMERY BUS BOYCOTT   49
   African Americans united to stop riding the buses   53
   The role of Dr. Martin Luther King Jr. in the boycott   56
   The impact on the city and the country   60

5. STANDING UP FOR CIVIL RIGHTS   63
   Working for the NAACP   66
   Speaking out for justice and equality   69
   How her courage inspired new laws   71

6. ROSA PARKS' LATER YEARS	75
Honored with awards	78
How Rosa Parks became a symbol of resistance	80
7. ROSA PARKS' LEGACY	83
The impact of her actions	85
Lessons kids can learn from her courage and determination	87
Conclusion	91
Glossary	97
Fun Facts	103
Discussion Questions	107

INTRODUCTION

Rosa Parks didn't set out to change the world, but that's exactly what happened. One choice, one moment, one decision to stay seated instead of giving up her bus seat sparked something much bigger than anyone could have expected. People had been fighting against unfair treatment for a long time, but her bravery on that December day in 1955 brought more people together in a powerful way.

During Rosa Parks' time, segregation was part of daily life. There were separate schools, separate restaurants, and even separate water fountains for Black and white people. It wasn't just about being separated—it was about being treated as less important. White people had access to better schools, better jobs, and more opportunities, while Black people were expected to accept whatever they were given, no matter how unfair it was.

One of the most frustrating parts of segregation was public transportation. Black passengers had to sit at the back of the bus, and if the front seats filled up, they had to give up their seats for white passengers. It didn't matter if they were tired, sick, or had been working all day. The rules were the rules. But just because something is a rule doesn't mean it's right.

Rosa Parks knew this. She had spent years speaking out against unfair treatment. She worked with the NAACP, an organization that fought for equal rights. She knew that people deserved to be treated with respect, no matter the color of their skin. That's why, when a bus driver told her to give up her seat, she refused. It wasn't because she was tired, as some stories say. It was because she was tired of giving in.

What happened next changed history. Rosa was arrested, and news spread quickly. People were upset —not just about what happened to her, but about what had been happening for years. Leaders like Dr. Martin Luther King Jr. helped organize the Montgomery Bus Boycott, where Black people stopped riding city buses. Without their money, the bus system struggled. After more than a year, the laws finally changed, proving that standing up—or in Rosa's case, sitting down—for what is right can lead to real change.

Rosa Parks became known as the "Mother of the Civil Rights Movement," but she didn't stop after the bus boycott. She kept fighting for justice throughout her life. She spoke out against unfair laws, helped people register to vote, and worked to make sure future generations would have better opportunities. She showed that even when things seem impossible, change is possible if enough people refuse to accept injustice.

Today, Rosa Parks is remembered as a hero, but she wasn't the only one who made a difference. Her story reminds us that anyone can take a stand against unfairness. It's not always easy, and sometimes it takes time, but even small actions can help make the world a fairer place. Rosa Parks wasn't famous when she made her decision, and she didn't have a big title or special power. What she did have was courage, and that made all the difference.

Her role in the Civil Rights Movement

The Civil Rights Movement was about much more than bus seats. It was about making sure all people, no matter their skin color, had the same rights and opportunities. Black Americans had been treated unfairly for a long time, and many laws in the South were designed to keep things that way. Schools were segregated, meaning Black children and white children couldn't attend the same schools. Black Americans were often blocked from voting, making it harder for them to have a say in their own communities. They faced discrimination when looking for jobs, housing, and even basic services.

Many people fought against these unfair laws, long before Rosa Parks took her stand. Organizations like the NAACP worked for years to challenge segregation and push for better treatment. Rosa Parks was part of that effort. Long before she made headlines, she was working behind the scenes, helping Black people register to vote, investigating cases where Black Americans had been treated unfairly, and pushing for change.

When she refused to give up her bus seat in 1955, it wasn't a random decision. It was a choice based on years of frustration and a belief that the rules had to change. Her arrest led to something much bigger: the Montgomery Bus Boycott. Black residents of Montgomery, Alabama, decided they had had enough. If buses wouldn't treat them fairly, they wouldn't ride them at all.

This wasn't easy. Many Black workers depended on buses to get to work. Walking miles each day was exhausting. Some people lost their jobs because they refused to give in. But they kept going. The boycott lasted for over a year, and it worked. The Supreme Court finally ruled that segregation on buses was unconstitutional. That victory showed people across the country that change was possible.

The success of the boycott gave strength to the Civil Rights Movement. It proved that ordinary people could make a difference. Rosa Parks became a powerful symbol of that idea. She traveled around the country, speaking about civil rights and inspiring others to take action. She worked with leaders like Martin Luther King Jr. and helped shape the movement's goals.

The fight wasn't just about buses. It was about education, voting rights, fair treatment, and equal opportunities. Rosa Parks spent her life working on these issues. Even after she moved to Detroit, she continued to be a voice for justice. She spoke against housing discrimination, helped young activists, and reminded people that the fight for equality wasn't over.

Laws changed because of the Civil Rights Movement, but it wasn't instant, and it wasn't easy. It took marches, protests, speeches, and court battles. It took courage from thousands of people, including Rosa Parks, who refused to accept an unfair system. Many of the rights that people have today exist because of the work done during that time.

1

GROWING UP IN THE SOUTH

Rosa Parks was born in Tuskegee, Alabama, in 1913, a time when life was very different for Black Americans. The South had strict segregation laws that kept Black and white people apart in almost every part of life. Schools, restaurants, and even drinking fountains were labeled "white" and "colored," and Black people were expected to follow rules that were designed to keep them from having the same opportunities as white people. It wasn't fair, but it was the way things had been for a long time.

Growing up in Alabama, Rosa Parks saw this unfairness everywhere. From a young age, she understood that being Black meant facing challenges that white children didn't have to think about.

It wasn't just about where she could sit or where she could go—it affected everything, from education to jobs to how people were treated in stores and on the street. Many Black families, including hers, worked hard to make a living while facing constant discrimination.

Her parents, James and Leona McCauley, knew how unfair the world could be, but they also believed in standing up for themselves. Her mother was a teacher who encouraged Rosa to value education, even though getting a good education was not easy for Black children. Her father, a carpenter, wanted better opportunities for his family, but he also understood that segregation made life harder. When Rosa was young, her parents separated, and she moved with her mother and younger brother, Sylvester, to Pine Level, Alabama, to live with her grandparents.

Life in Pine Level was shaped by the racial divide in the South. White children rode buses to school, while Black children had to walk, no matter how far or how bad the weather was. Schools for Black children often had fewer resources, older books, and fewer teachers. Even though Rosa Parks wanted to learn, she saw that education was not equal. Black students were expected to settle for less.

Her family didn't accept those rules quietly. Her grandfather, a former enslaved person, taught her about the struggles Black people had faced for generations. He told her about the importance of standing up for what was right, even when it was difficult. Rosa saw his determination and learned that strength wasn't just about speaking loudly—it was about refusing to accept what was wrong.

Because of segregation, Black families had to create their own communities where they could support each other. Churches, schools, and family homes became places where people could come together, share stories, and encourage one another. Rosa Parks grew up in one of these communities, surrounded by people who believed in fighting for fairness. Even though laws were against them, they found ways to take care of one another.

One of the biggest lessons Rosa Parks learned as a child was that discrimination wasn't just about rules—it was about power. White people in the South had the power to control what Black people could and couldn't do. That power showed up in small ways, like who got to drink from the best water fountains, and in big ways, like who could vote or get a good job. It was frustrating to see people treated unfairly just because of their skin color, but

Rosa Parks knew she wasn't alone in feeling that way.

She also learned that speaking up could be dangerous. Black people who challenged segregation could lose their jobs, be arrested, or even be attacked. The Ku Klux Klan, a violent group that targeted Black families, was active in Alabama, and many Black families, including Rosa's, had to be careful about how they acted in public. Her grandfather often stayed up at night with a shotgun, ready to protect his family if necessary. Even though Rosa Parks was just a child, she understood that unfairness wasn't just about rules—it was about safety and survival.

Life in the segregated South

Growing up in Alabama during the early 1900s meant living under strict segregation laws. Everything in daily life was divided by race—schools, churches, restaurants, movie theaters, public transportation, even drinking fountains. These rules were known as Jim Crow laws, and they weren't just about separating Black and white people. They were designed to keep Black Americans in a lower position in society, making sure they had fewer opportunities and less power.

Black children in the South quickly learned that the world wasn't fair. They saw it in their schools, which had fewer books and supplies than white schools. They saw it in their neighborhoods, which had dirt roads while white neighborhoods had paved streets. They saw it in stores, where Black customers were expected to wait until all the white customers had been helped.

Rosa Parks saw these things too. She knew that life was harder for Black families, not because they weren't smart or hardworking, but because the system was built to keep them from getting ahead. Schools for Black children were often small and overcrowded, with old textbooks that had been passed down from white schools. Many Black children had to work on farms or take jobs at a young age to help support their families, making it harder to get an education. Some never finished school at all because they were needed at home.

Transportation was another daily reminder that Black people were treated unfairly. City buses had separate sections for Black and white passengers. Black riders had to enter through the back door and sit in the back rows. If the white section filled up, Black passengers were expected to give up their seats, even if they had paid for their ride just like everyone else. It didn't matter if they were elderly, sick, or carrying heavy bags. White passengers always had the priority.

Trains followed similar rules. Black passengers had their own waiting rooms at train stations, which were usually smaller and less comfortable than the ones for white passengers. On long trips, they were given separate train cars that were often older and not as well-maintained. Even though they were paying customers, they were made to feel like they didn't belong.

Segregation wasn't just about where people could sit or go. It affected jobs too. Black workers were often paid less than white workers, even if they did the same work. Many businesses wouldn't even hire Black employees for certain positions, no matter how qualified they were. Some jobs were completely off-limits, and if a Black person did find a good job, they could be fired for speaking out against unfair treatment.

For Rosa Parks and her family, life under segregation wasn't just frustrating—it was exhausting. Every day, they had to follow rules that reminded them they weren't treated equally. They had to be careful about what they said in public because speaking out could lead to trouble. Black people who challenged segregation could be harassed, arrested, or even attacked.

Even though these laws were unfair, Black communities found ways to support each other. Families looked out for one another, sharing food, clothes, and advice. Churches played a big role, not just as places of worship but as gathering spaces where people could talk about their struggles and plan for a better future. Schools might not have had the best supplies, but teachers worked hard to make sure their students learned as much as possible.

Rosa Parks was raised in this kind of community. She learned from an early age that while the laws were unfair, her worth was not determined by them. Her family, her teachers, and the people around her reminded her that she was just as smart and capable as anyone else. She was taught that even though the system was against her, she didn't have to accept it quietly.

Learning about discrimination from an early age

Rosa Parks didn't have to wait until she was older to understand that the world around her was unfair.

From the time she was a child, she saw the ways that Black people were treated differently from white people. It wasn't something she had to be taught in a classroom—she saw it every day, in the streets, in stores, in schools, and even in the way people spoke to each other.

One of the first things she noticed was that white children and Black children weren't treated the same, even when they lived in the same town. White children had new schoolbooks, clean classrooms, and school buses that took them to and from school. Black children had to walk, even if the journey was long and tiring. There were no buses for them. Some children had to wake up extra early just to make it to school on time because their schools were farther away, often placed in locations that weren't as well maintained. Even when they got to school, the buildings were smaller, and the supplies were old.

Stores had separate entrances for Black and white customers. Black people weren't allowed to try on clothes before buying them. If they wanted to buy a hat, they had to guess if it would fit because store owners didn't want Black customers touching items that white customers might later purchase. Restaurants had separate sections, or they refused to serve Black customers at all. If a Black family wanted to eat out, they had to find a business that welcomed them, which wasn't always easy.

One of the most frustrating things was how Black people were expected to behave around white people. A Black person couldn't disagree with a white person without risking serious trouble. If a Black person was walking down the sidewalk and a white person approached, they were expected to step aside and lower their head. If a Black person spoke out against unfair treatment, they could lose their job, be arrested, or face even worse consequences.

Even children had to be careful. A Black child could get in trouble just for playing in the wrong area or speaking to a white child in a way that was considered too friendly. There were rules, both written and unwritten, that controlled every part of life. Black people were expected to follow them without question, no matter how unfair they were.

Rosa Parks grew up hearing stories about what could happen if someone broke those rules. She knew that people who stood up against segregation often faced punishment. She also saw people being treated unfairly right in front of her.

She saw it on public transportation, where Black passengers had to sit in the back of the bus while white passengers sat in the front. Even if there were empty seats in the white section, a Black passenger couldn't sit there. If the bus became crowded, Black riders were expected to give up their seats. If they refused, they could be arrested. It didn't matter if they were tired or had been working all day. The rules were designed to keep Black people in their place.

She saw it in how her family had to work harder for less. Many jobs were only available to white workers, and even when Black workers did the same jobs, they were often paid less. Some jobs were only open to Black workers if white people didn't want them. A Black worker could be fired without warning, and there weren't many options for speaking out about unfair treatment.

Even voting was difficult. Black people had the right to vote, but there were rules in place to make it almost impossible. They had to take difficult tests, pay fees, and go through other obstacles that white people didn't have to face. Some Black people who tried to register to vote were threatened or attacked.

Rosa Parks' family didn't just accept these things without question. Her grandfather, a former enslaved person, taught her about the struggles that Black people had faced for generations. He told her about slavery, about the fight for freedom, and about the unfair system that still existed. He didn't want Rosa to be afraid, but he wanted her to understand the truth about the world she lived in.

Her mother also made sure she understood the importance of education. Even though Black schools weren't as well-funded as white schools, her mother encouraged her to learn as much as she could. Education was one of the few things that could help Black children build a better future, even if the odds were against them.

Churches were also important places for learning. Black churches were more than just places to worship. They were places where people could come together, share information, and support one another. Many churches taught their members that they deserved to be treated with respect, even if the laws said otherwise.

Rosa's love for education

Rosa Parks valued education from an early age, even though getting an education as a Black child in Alabama was not easy. She grew up in a time when schools were segregated, and Black children were given far fewer resources than white children.

Despite these obstacles, she loved to learn. She was curious about the world, eager to read, and determined to make the most of every opportunity to gain knowledge.

Her mother, Leona McCauley, was a teacher, and she made sure that Rosa understood how important school was. She encouraged her to study hard, to do her best, and to never let unfair rules stop her from learning. Education was one of the few things that could open doors for Black children, even in a society that tried to hold them back. Rosa Parks took that lesson seriously.

Going to school, however, was not as simple as showing up and learning. Black children were expected to deal with conditions that white children never had to face. Schools for Black students had fewer supplies, older books, and often, overcrowded classrooms. The buildings were small, sometimes run-down, and lacked basic necessities like enough desks or proper heating.

While white children were provided with new textbooks and well-maintained schools, Black students had to make do with whatever was left over. The books Rosa Parks and her classmates used were often hand-me-downs from white schools. These books were sometimes falling apart, filled with notes or markings, and missing pages. It sent a clear message that Black students were not given the same importance as white students.

Getting to school was another challenge. White children had buses to take them to and from school each day, but Black children had to walk. It didn't matter if their school was miles away or if the weather was bad—there was no transportation provided for them. Rosa Parks, like many other Black children, had to walk long distances to get to school.

Despite these difficulties, she loved learning. She enjoyed reading, and she worked hard to do well in her classes. She didn't let the unfair conditions take away her enthusiasm for education. She saw school as a way to grow, to gain knowledge, and to prepare for a better future.

She first attended a small school in Pine Level, Alabama, where her mother taught. Even though the school was not well-funded, the teachers cared deeply about their students. They encouraged them to take their education seriously, knowing that it was one of the few tools they had to fight against a system that tried to keep them in a lower position.

As Rosa Parks got older, she wanted to continue her education beyond the small school in Pine Level.

She was accepted into the Montgomery Industrial School for Girls, a school that focused on providing Black girls with a good education and useful skills. The school's teachers believed in hard work and discipline, and they encouraged their students to aim high.

The Montgomery Industrial School was run by white women who wanted to help Black girls receive an education, but even this school faced difficulties. The local white community did not like the idea of Black children receiving a quality education, and the school sometimes faced threats. But Rosa Parks kept going. She wanted to learn, and she wasn't going to let anything stop her.

She continued her studies and later enrolled at Booker T. Washington High School, a school that provided more advanced education for Black students. She was determined to finish, but life had other plans. Her mother and grandmother became sick, and Rosa Parks had to leave school to take care of them. She didn't drop out because she wanted to —she did it because her family needed her.

2

LIFE UNDER SEGREGATION

Living under segregation meant that Black people and white people were kept apart in nearly every part of daily life. It wasn't just about where someone could sit on a bus or which school they could attend. Segregation controlled where people lived, what jobs they could have, how they were treated in stores and restaurants, and even where they could get medical care. These laws and rules were designed to remind Black Americans that they were considered second-class citizens.

Public places were divided by race. There were separate water fountains, separate bathrooms, separate waiting rooms at train stations, and separate seating sections in theaters. In many cases, the spaces reserved for Black people were smaller, older, and not well-maintained. White businesses and services received more funding, while Black communities had to make do with whatever was left.

Restaurants either refused to serve Black customers or required them to sit in a separate section, usually at the back or outside. If a Black person wanted to order food, they sometimes had to go to a side window and take their meal to go because they weren't allowed to sit inside. Some stores wouldn't even let Black customers try on clothes before buying them. The idea was that once a Black person touched an item, white customers wouldn't want it anymore.

Transportation was another daily reminder of segregation. Black passengers on buses had to sit in the back, even if there were open seats at the front. If all the white seats were full, a Black passenger could be forced to give up their seat, even if they had paid the same fare. Train stations had separate waiting rooms, and train cars for Black passengers were often smaller and less comfortable than those for white passengers.

Schools were also segregated, and the differences between them were obvious. White schools were newer, larger, and had more resources, including up-to-date textbooks, well-trained teachers, and science labs. Black schools were often overcrowded, underfunded, and filled with used books that were years old. The message was clear—white students were given the best opportunities, while Black students were expected to accept whatever they were given.

Workplaces were no different. Many companies refused to hire Black workers for anything other than low-paying jobs. If a Black worker and a white worker had the same job, the Black worker was usually paid less. Even highly skilled Black workers often struggled to find jobs that matched their abilities. They were blocked from certain professions, and if they spoke out about unfair treatment, they could be fired or even threatened.

Even something as basic as healthcare was affected by segregation. Black people were often denied treatment at white hospitals, and if they were treated, it was usually in separate wings or basement rooms. Black doctors and nurses had limited places where they could practice, and Black patients often had to travel long distances to see a doctor who would care for them.

Voting was another right that was technically legal but made nearly impossible for many Black Americans. Segregationists used poll taxes, literacy tests, and intimidation to keep Black people from voting. Some Black citizens were forced to answer impossible questions, like guessing the number of jellybeans in a jar, before being allowed to register. Others were threatened with losing their jobs or being harmed if they tried to vote.

Daily life under segregation meant constantly being reminded that the system was designed to favor white people. It wasn't just about separate spaces—it was about power. The laws made it difficult for Black Americans to advance in society, no matter how hard they worked. They weren't just treated unfairly; they were expected to accept it.

Different rules for Black and white people

Segregation didn't just mean that Black people and white people had to use separate schools, buses, and businesses. It also meant that they were treated completely differently under the law. The rules were not the same for everyone. White people had more rights, more freedom, and more opportunities, while Black people were expected to follow strict rules that limited their lives in almost every way. These rules weren't just about keeping things separate—they were about making sure that

Black Americans remained in a lower position in society.

Laws made it difficult for Black people to own land, vote, or even defend themselves in court. A white person could say anything against a Black person, and in many cases, they would automatically be believed, no matter what the truth was. A Black person who was accused of a crime could be arrested without real evidence, while a white person who harmed a Black person often faced no punishment at all.

Even the way people spoke to each other was controlled by segregation. Black people were expected to show constant respect toward white people, even when they weren't being treated with respect in return. A Black person couldn't call a white person by their first name unless they were given permission, but a white person could call a Black adult "boy" or "girl," no matter how old they were. If a Black person failed to show the level of "respect" expected of them, they could be punished, threatened, or even attacked.

There were also rules about how Black and white people could interact in public. A Black person couldn't shake hands with a white person because it suggested they were equals. If a Black person was walking down the sidewalk and a white person approached, the Black person was expected to step aside. If a Black person entered a store, they often had to wait until all white customers had been helped before they could be served, no matter how long they had been waiting.

Restaurants, hotels, and movie theaters either refused to serve Black customers or forced them into separate areas. Even places that were open to both races had different rules. A Black person could enter a store but not try on clothes before buying them. A Black family could go to a park but could only use certain areas, and those areas were often smaller or not well maintained.

Transportation had its own set of unfair rules. On buses, Black passengers had to sit in the back. If the front seats were empty, they still couldn't use them. If the white section was full, Black passengers had to give up their seats and stand, even if they had paid the same fare. If a Black person refused, they could be arrested or beaten.

Even in hospitals, the rules were different. Black patients were often given worse treatment, if they were treated at all. Some hospitals refused to admit Black patients, even in emergencies. Black doctors and nurses had limited places where they could work, which meant that many Black communities struggled to get medical care.

The rules also affected Black businesses. Many banks refused to give loans to Black business owners, making it difficult to open or expand a business. If a Black business did become successful, white customers often refused to shop there, and some white business owners tried to put them out of business.

Education was one of the biggest areas where the rules were unfair. Black schools received less funding, fewer books, and little support from the government. Even when Black students worked hard, they were told they could never have the same jobs or opportunities as white students. Many colleges wouldn't admit Black students at all, and even those that did often kept them separate from white students.

The unfairness of public transportation

Public transportation, schools, and businesses were all affected by segregation, and none of them treated Black Americans fairly. These were not just minor inconveniences—they were daily reminders that society was set up to keep Black people in a lower position. The rules were not about safety or organization; they were about control. White people were given better services, better resources, and more opportunities, while Black people were expected to accept whatever was left over.

Public transportation was one of the clearest examples of this unfairness. Black passengers paid the same fare as white passengers, yet they were forced to sit in the back of the bus. The first few rows were reserved for white passengers, even if they were empty. If the white section filled up, Black riders were expected to give up their seats. Bus drivers had the power to make Black passengers move or even force them off the bus if they refused to follow the rules. If a Black person protested, they could be arrested or worse.

Getting on the bus was also humiliating. In some cities, Black passengers had to pay their fare at the front, then step off and re-enter through the back door. There were times when drivers pulled away before Black passengers could get back on, leaving them stranded even though they had already paid. These rules were designed to remind Black people that they were not considered equal, even in something as simple as taking a bus to work or school.

Trains were no better. Black passengers were

given separate waiting rooms at train stations, which were smaller and less comfortable than those for white passengers. On the trains themselves, Black passengers were placed in cars that were often older, dirtier, and poorly maintained. It didn't matter if they had a ticket just like everyone else—they were still treated as less important.

Schools were another place where segregation created deep unfairness. White schools were newer, larger, and better funded. They had well-trained teachers, science labs, libraries, and up-to-date textbooks. Black schools were often run-down buildings with broken desks, outdated books, and too many students crammed into small classrooms. In many cases, Black children didn't even have real school buildings; they had to learn in churches or community centers because their towns didn't want to spend money on schools for them.

Teachers at Black schools worked hard to educate their students, but they had fewer resources. The government spent more money on white schools than on Black schools, making it clear that Black children were not a priority. Even though Black students were just as smart and capable, they were given fewer tools to succeed.

Higher education was even more difficult. Many

colleges and universities would not admit Black students at all. If they did, they kept them in separate classrooms or housing. Scholarships were harder to get, and career opportunities after graduation were limited because many companies would not hire Black workers for well-paying jobs.

Businesses followed the same unfair rules. Many restaurants, hotels, and stores refused to serve Black customers. If a Black person wanted to eat at a restaurant, they often had to take their food to go because they were not allowed to sit inside. Hotels turned away Black travelers, forcing them to find other places to sleep, even if they had the money to pay for a room.

Even in stores, the discrimination was obvious. Black customers were expected to wait until all white customers had been helped, even if they had been standing in line first. They were not allowed to try on clothes before buying them, meaning they had to guess if something would fit. Store owners didn't want Black customers touching items that white customers might later purchase.

Black-owned businesses struggled to survive because they faced extra challenges. Banks often refused to give loans to Black business owners, making it harder to start or expand a business. Many white customers refused to shop at Black-owned stores, and white business owners sometimes pressured suppliers not to sell to Black store owners. Even when a Black business was successful, it could be targeted by racist laws or violent attacks.

These unfair rules weren't just about keeping things separate. They were designed to remind Black people that they had fewer rights and fewer choices. They affected every part of life—how people got to work, where they went to school, and whether they could shop, eat, or even travel freely. The system was built to make sure Black Americans stayed at a disadvantage, no matter how hard they worked or how much they tried to improve their lives.

The Montgomery bus system

The Montgomery bus system was supposed to be a public service, available to everyone who paid a fare. But for Black passengers, riding the bus was a daily reminder that they were not treated equally. Every part of the experience—from getting on the bus to finding a seat to dealing with drivers—was shaped by unfair rules that put white passengers first. These rules were not based on logic or fairness. They were designed to keep Black people in their place, even in something as simple as public transportation.

Black riders made up the majority of bus passengers in Montgomery. Many Black workers depended on buses to get to their jobs because they couldn't afford cars. Despite this, they were treated as if their presence was a burden rather than an essential part of the system. They were expected to pay the same fare as white passengers, yet they were given worse treatment in return.

Seating was strictly segregated. The first few rows of seats at the front of the bus were reserved for white passengers. Black passengers had to sit in the back, even if there were empty seats in the white section. If the front filled up and more white passengers got on, Black passengers had to give up their seats and move farther back. If the bus was completely full, Black riders had to stand or leave the bus entirely, while white passengers remained seated.

The process of getting on the bus was another way that segregation laws made life harder for Black passengers. In Montgomery, Black riders were expected to pay at the front of the bus, then step off and re-enter through the back door. This rule was humiliating enough, but some bus drivers used it as an opportunity to show their power. There were times when a Black passenger paid their fare at the front, stepped off to walk around to the back door, and the driver pulled away before they could get back on. This meant they had paid for a ride they never got, and there was nothing they could do about it.

Bus drivers had full control over who could ride and how they were treated. Many of them were openly racist, using their position to bully Black passengers. If a Black passenger didn't move quickly enough when told to give up their seat, the driver could call the police to have them arrested. Some drivers even carried guns to intimidate passengers. Complaints from Black riders were ignored or dismissed, and there was no real way to challenge the treatment they received.

Black passengers were expected to follow the rules without question, but white passengers were not held to the same standard. White riders could take any open seat they wanted, even in sections designated for Black passengers. If a Black passenger was already sitting there, they were expected to move without argument. If a Black person dared to challenge these rules, they risked arrest, violence, or losing their job.

For years, Black community leaders tried to address the unfair treatment of bus passengers. They filed complaints, wrote letters, and asked city officials to change the policies. But nothing happened. The city leaders and bus company officials refused to listen, and the unfair rules remained in place.

3

THE DAY THAT CHANGED HISTORY

Rosa Parks had been riding the Montgomery buses for years. She knew the rules. Every Black passenger did. They knew which section to sit in, they knew that their seat was never really theirs, and they knew that if a bus driver told them to move, arguing could lead to arrest—or worse. Nothing about December 1, 1955, seemed different at first. It was an ordinary day, and Rosa Parks had no reason to expect it would end any differently than the ones before it.

The day had been long. She had spent hours at her job as a seamstress, stitching and repairing clothing for the Montgomery Fair department store. Like many Black workers, she put in full days of hard work but was paid less than white employees doing the same job. The bus was how she got home, the same as it was for thousands of other Black residents in Montgomery. It wasn't a pleasant experience, but it was necessary.

When she boarded the Cleveland Avenue bus, she found a seat in the section designated for Black passengers. This area was toward the middle of the bus, behind the seats reserved for white riders. The first few rows at the front were empty, but that didn't matter. Black passengers were not allowed to sit there, even if no white passengers needed the seats. The rule had been clear for years: Black riders were expected to sit in their assigned section, and if more white passengers boarded and the front seats filled up, the Black riders in the middle section had to move farther back—or give up their seats entirely.

The bus continued its route, stopping to pick up more passengers. White passengers filled the front section, and then more boarded, standing in the aisle. The bus driver noticed that the first few rows of the Black section were now occupied, meaning white passengers would have to stand unless someone moved. He told the Black passengers in the row where Rosa Parks was sitting to get up and make room.

This was not the first time this had happened. It

was a normal part of bus rides in Montgomery. Black passengers had no choice but to comply, no matter how unfair it was. Many had been arrested before for refusing. Some had been beaten. The system was designed to remind Black riders that they were not seen as equals.

Rosa Parks did not move.

The others in her row stood up and moved toward the back, following the rule that had been forced upon them for so long. But Rosa Parks remained in her seat. She wasn't being loud. She wasn't trying to cause trouble. She was just staying where she was.

The bus driver noticed immediately. He told her to move. She refused.

This was a dangerous moment. Black passengers were not allowed to challenge bus drivers. They were given the power to enforce segregation however they saw fit, and they often called the police when Black passengers did not obey immediately.

The driver asked again, louder this time. Rosa Parks still refused.

She was tired, but not just in the way someone is tired after a long day at work. She was tired of the constant disrespect. Tired of being treated as less important. Tired of rules that forced Black people to move, to wait, to step aside, to accept less. She had followed these rules her whole life, and she knew that following them had never made things better.

The bus driver warned her that if she didn't move, he would call the police. She told him to go ahead.

It was not the first time a Black passenger had been arrested for refusing to give up a seat, but something about this moment felt different. Rosa Parks was not a random passenger. She had been involved in the fight for civil rights for years. She had worked with the NAACP, helping document cases of Black people being mistreated by the law. She knew the risks of what she was doing. But she also knew the importance of making a stand—or, in this case, staying seated.

Arrest and consequences

The police arrived quickly. They had been called for this kind of situation before. In Montgomery, it was not unusual for Black passengers to be arrested for refusing to move on a bus. The system was designed to work this way—bus drivers had the authority to call the police if any Black passenger didn't follow their commands. When the officers stepped onto the bus, they expected Rosa Parks to do what most people did in these situations: get up, apologize, and try to avoid trouble.

She did none of those things.

She remained seated, looking straight ahead, calm but firm. She had done nothing wrong. She had paid her fare, taken her seat, and simply refused to give it up for a white passenger. The officers didn't see it that way. They saw her as a problem that needed to be removed.

They asked her again to move. She refused.

There was no shouting. There was no fight. But there was force. The officers ordered her to stand, placed her under arrest, and led her off the bus. As she stepped onto the sidewalk, people turned to watch. Some Black passengers lowered their heads, afraid to show too much interest. They had seen what happened when people interfered in arrests like this. Others took mental notes of what was happening, knowing they would later tell their families about what they had witnessed.

She was taken to the local police station, where she was fingerprinted and processed like a criminal. Her charge was "disorderly conduct." The police treated her as if she had committed a serious crime, even though all she had done was refuse to give up her seat. She was placed in a jail cell to wait.

News of her arrest spread quickly. The Black community in Montgomery had been dealing with the city's unfair bus rules for years, and many were angry that yet another person had been arrested for simply wanting to sit where they had paid to sit. But Rosa Parks was not just any passenger. She was well-known and respected, especially among those involved in civil rights efforts. She had worked for the NAACP, helped register Black voters, and fought against injustice long before she sat on that bus. Her arrest was not going to be ignored.

A phone call was made to E.D. Nixon, a local civil rights leader who had been looking for a case to challenge segregation in Montgomery. When he heard that Rosa Parks had been arrested, he knew this moment was important. He contacted a local attorney and arranged for her bail. After several hours in jail, she was released, but her fight was just beginning.

The next step was the courtroom. She was charged with violating the city's segregation laws, and her trial was scheduled quickly. The laws were not on her side. The legal system in Montgomery, like much of the South, had been designed to keep segregation in place. But she and the people supporting her knew that fighting back was necessary. They would not let her arrest be just another forgotten case.

How Rosa's actions sparked a movement

The arrest of Rosa Parks was not the first time a Black passenger had been removed from a bus in Montgomery. It had happened before. Many times. People had been fined, jailed, and even beaten for refusing to give up their seats. Most cases ended the same way—an arrest, a small protest, and then things returned to how they had always been. But something was different this time.

Rosa Parks was not just another passenger. She had spent years working for civil rights. She knew how the legal system worked. She understood how segregation laws were designed to keep Black people in a lower position. When she was arrested, she was not simply taken away in silence. She had connections. She had a community that was ready to act.

The news spread quickly. Black leaders in Montgomery knew they could not let this moment pass without taking action. People were tired of the daily humiliation on the buses. Tired of being forced to give up their seats. Tired of the rules that only benefited white passengers. Rosa Parks' arrest became the moment when people decided they would not just complain about the unfairness—they would do something about it.

E.D. Nixon, a longtime civil rights activist, was one of the first to step in. He saw Rosa Parks' case as an opportunity to challenge segregation in a way that the city could not ignore. He met with local ministers, educators, and community leaders to discuss a strategy. The idea was simple but powerful—Black residents would stop riding the buses.

The city's bus system depended on Black passengers. They were the majority of the riders, paying their fares every day, keeping the buses running. Without them, the system would struggle. If enough Black residents refused to ride, the city would feel the impact. It would send a message that they were not willing to accept second-class treatment anymore.

Plans for a boycott moved quickly. Flyers were printed and handed out in Black neighborhoods, churches, and schools. People were asked to stop riding the buses on Monday, December 5—the day of Rosa Parks' trial. If it worked, they would continue the protest for as long as it took.

Not everyone believed it would succeed. Some worried that too many people relied on the buses to get to work. Others feared that those who participated would lose their jobs. But when Monday arrived, it became clear that something powerful was happening.

The buses were nearly empty. Black residents walked instead of riding. Some carpooled with friends and neighbors. Taxi drivers, many of them Black, lowered their fares to help people get to work. Employers noticed that their Black workers were late or missing entirely. The city noticed that bus stops were quiet, and the bus company noticed its profits were shrinking.

The boycott had begun, and it was working.

What started as a one-day protest turned into something much bigger. The Montgomery Bus Boycott stretched on for weeks, then months. Every day, Black residents continued to walk, refusing to support a system that treated them as less than equal. They faced threats, harassment, and even violence, but they did not give in.

As the boycott gained national attention, more leaders stepped forward to help organize the movement. A young minister named Martin Luther King Jr. emerged as a key figure. He spoke at meetings, encouraged people to stay strong, and helped guide the protest forward. Under his leadership, the boycott became more than just about buses—it became part of the larger fight for civil rights across the country.

Rosa Parks' decision to stay seated had turned into something far bigger than one person refusing to move. It had sparked a movement that would change history. The fight against segregation had been going on for years, but her arrest gave it new momentum. It showed that peaceful resistance could be powerful. It showed that people working together could challenge unfair laws.

4

THE MONTGOMERY BUS BOYCOTT

News of Rosa Parks' arrest spread quickly. By the next morning, people were already talking about what had happened. It wasn't just that another Black passenger had been arrested for refusing to give up their seat—people were outraged because it was Rosa Parks. She was well-respected in Montgomery, known for her work in the community and her involvement with the NAACP. If someone like her could be arrested for simply sitting in a seat she had paid for, then no Black person was safe from the city's unfair bus system.

Leaders in the Black community knew that something had to be done. Rosa Parks' arrest was not just another incident. It was an opportunity to take a stand against the constant mistreatment of Black bus riders. The idea of a bus boycott had been talked about before, but now, with Rosa Parks' arrest fresh in everyone's mind, there was momentum to make it happen.

E.D. Nixon, a longtime civil rights leader in Montgomery, wasted no time. He called a meeting with other Black leaders, including local ministers and educators. They decided to organize a one-day boycott of the Montgomery buses. On Monday, December 5—the day of Rosa Parks' trial—Black residents would refuse to ride the buses.

The plan needed to reach as many people as possible. Over the weekend, volunteers worked quickly, printing and handing out flyers in churches, barber shops, grocery stores, and schools. The message was clear: do not ride the buses on Monday. Walk, carpool, or take a Black-owned taxi service, but do not give the city a single penny in bus fare.

Word of the boycott spread throughout Montgomery's Black neighborhoods. People talked about it at dinner tables, in churches, and on street corners. Some were nervous. Others were excited. Many had been waiting for a moment like this, a chance to take a stand against the unfair rules that had controlled their lives for too long.

Not everyone believed the boycott would work. Some worried that too many people depended on the buses to get to work. Others feared there would be punishment for those who participated. The city's white leaders did not take Black protests seriously, and there were concerns about what might happen if the boycott failed.

Monday morning arrived, and the results were undeniable. Black passengers made up the majority of bus riders in Montgomery, and without them, the buses were nearly empty. Many people walked miles to work, determined to show that they would not support a system that treated them unfairly. Black taxi drivers helped by lowering their fares to match the cost of a bus ride, making it easier for people to get around without using the bus system.

The boycott had begun, and it was more successful than anyone expected. Montgomery's white leaders noticed immediately. Bus stops that were usually crowded were now quiet. Bus drivers drove mostly empty buses through the city, collecting only a fraction of the usual fares.

At first, city officials believed the boycott would not last. They assumed that Black residents would grow tired of walking and return to the buses within a few days. But that didn't happen. People were willing to make sacrifices. They arranged carpools, rode bicycles, and even rode horses and mules when necessary. They found creative ways to avoid using the bus system, and each day that passed made it clearer that the boycott was not going to end quickly.

The Black community in Montgomery stood together in a way that city officials had not expected. Churches held meetings to encourage people to stay strong. Volunteers organized transportation systems to make sure workers could still get to their jobs. The longer the boycott lasted, the more people became involved.

The white leaders of Montgomery responded with anger. They saw the boycott as a threat to the city's authority. White business owners were upset because they relied on Black customers, and if workers couldn't get to their jobs, businesses suffered. City officials tried to force people back onto the buses by making it illegal for Black-owned taxi services to charge lower fares. Some police officers stopped Black carpool drivers and gave them tickets, hoping to make it harder for people to get around.

African Americans united to stop riding the buses

Leaders in the Black community knew that something had to be done. Rosa Parks' arrest was not just another incident. It was an opportunity to take a stand against the constant mistreatment of Black bus riders. The idea of a bus boycott had been talked about before, but now, with Rosa Parks' arrest fresh in everyone's mind, there was momentum to make it happen.

E.D. NIXON, a longtime civil rights leader in Montgomery, wasted no time. He called a meeting with other Black leaders, including local ministers and educators. They decided to organize a one-day boycott of the Montgomery buses. On Monday, December 5—the day of Rosa Parks' trial—Black residents would refuse to ride the buses.

THE PLAN NEEDED to reach as many people as possible. Over the weekend, volunteers worked quickly, printing and handing out flyers in churches, barber shops, grocery stores, and schools. The message was clear: do not ride the buses on Monday. Walk, carpool, or take a Black-owned taxi service, but do not give the city a single penny in bus fare.

Word of the boycott spread throughout Montgomery's Black neighborhoods. People talked about it at dinner tables, in churches, and on street corners. Some were nervous. Others were excited. Many had been waiting for a moment like this, a chance to take a stand against the unfair rules that had controlled their lives for too long.

Not everyone believed the boycott would work. Some worried that too many people depended on the buses to get to work. Others feared there would be punishment for those who participated. The city's white leaders did not take Black protests seriously, and there were concerns about what might happen if the boycott failed.

Monday morning arrived, and the results were undeniable. Black passengers made up the majority of bus riders in Montgomery, and without them, the buses were nearly empty. Many people walked miles to work, determined to show that they would not support a system that treated them unfairly. Black taxi drivers helped by lowering their fares to match the cost of a bus ride, making it easier for people to get around without using the bus system.

THE BOYCOTT HAD BEGUN, and it was more successful than anyone expected. Montgomery's white leaders noticed immediately. Bus stops that were usually crowded were now quiet. Bus drivers drove mostly empty buses through the city, collecting only a fraction of the usual fares.

AT FIRST, city officials believed the boycott would not last. They assumed that Black residents would grow tired of walking and return to the buses within a few days. But that didn't happen. People were willing to make sacrifices. They arranged carpools, rode bicycles, and even rode horses and mules when necessary. They found creative ways to avoid using the bus system, and each day that passed made it clearer that the boycott was not going to end quickly.

. . .

THE BLACK COMMUNITY in Montgomery stood together in a way that city officials had not expected. Churches held meetings to encourage people to stay strong. Volunteers organized transportation systems to make sure workers could still get to their jobs. The longer the boycott lasted, the more people became involved.

THE WHITE LEADERS of Montgomery responded with anger. They saw the boycott as a threat to the city's authority. White business owners were upset because they relied on Black customers, and if workers couldn't get to their jobs, businesses suffered. City officials tried to force people back onto the buses by making it illegal for Black-owned taxi services to charge lower fares. Some police officers stopped Black carpool drivers and gave them tickets, hoping to make it harder for people to get around.

The role of Dr. Martin Luther King Jr. in the boycott

At the time, Dr. King was only 26 years old. He was a young minister at Dexter Avenue Baptist Church in Montgomery, a city he had moved to just a year earlier. He was well-educated and had studied theology and philosophy, but he was not yet well-known outside of Montgomery. That would soon change.

Black leaders in the city knew the boycott needed organization. It wasn't enough for people to simply stop riding the buses—they needed a plan to keep the movement going and to make sure their message was heard. A meeting was called to discuss who would lead this effort. The group decided to form the Montgomery Improvement Association (MIA) to oversee the boycott, and they needed a president.

Many of the older leaders in Montgomery had been fighting segregation for years, but this moment required someone fresh, someone who could bring energy to the movement. They wanted a leader who was smart, well-spoken, and respected. Dr. King was relatively new to Montgomery, but he was already admired for his powerful sermons and strong moral beliefs. When his name was suggested, people quickly agreed.

At first, he hesitated. Leading the boycott would put him in danger. Challenging segregation was not just about speeches and meetings—it could lead to threats, violence, and even arrest. But he knew the moment was bigger than his own fears. The boycott needed a leader who could inspire people to stay strong, and he accepted the role.

The first major test of his leadership came on December 5, 1955, the night of Rosa Parks' trial. Thousands of Black residents packed into the Holt Street Baptist Church for a mass meeting. They wanted to know what would happen next. Would the boycott continue? Would they give up? What was the plan?

Dr. King stood before them and gave a speech that would define the movement. He spoke about injustice, dignity, and the power of nonviolence. He told the crowd that the time for waiting was over and that the boycott was not just about buses—it was about equality. He did not shout or threaten. Instead, he spoke calmly and confidently, explaining why their cause was just. His words electrified the room. People left that meeting more determined than ever to continue the protest.

Under Dr. King's leadership, the boycott stayed strong. He helped organize carpools so that workers could still get to their jobs. He encouraged church leaders to keep their communities motivated. He reminded people that nonviolence was the best way to win. While the city's white leaders tried to crush the boycott through intimidation and legal pressure, he urged protesters to remain peaceful.

The response to his leadership was not always positive. White city officials and segregationists saw him as a threat. Soon after he became the public face of the boycott, he received his first death threat. More followed. He was arrested on charges of disrupting the peace, even though the boycott was entirely peaceful. His home was bombed while his wife and young child were inside.

Each time he was attacked, he refused to back down. Instead, he continued to speak, organize, and encourage people to keep going. His leadership gave the boycott not just structure but a sense of purpose. It was no longer just about Montgomery—it was about something much bigger.

As the boycott stretched from weeks into months, his influence grew. Reporters came to Montgomery to cover the protest, and Dr. King's speeches and actions caught the attention of people across the country. He became one of the most recognized voices of the Civil Rights Movement.

The impact on the city and the country

The city of Montgomery quickly felt the effects. The bus system had relied heavily on Black passengers, who made up about 75 percent of its riders. Without them, buses were nearly empty. Drivers still ran their routes, but with rows of open seats. The fares that once kept the system running started to dry up. Each day that passed without Black riders hurt the city financially. Officials expected the boycott to fall apart within days, but it didn't. People found other ways to get around, and the buses remained nearly empty.

The loss of money was only part of the impact. The city's white leaders were furious that Black residents were refusing to back down. Segregation had existed in Montgomery for decades, and the idea that Black workers, students, and churchgoers were resisting the system made those in power uneasy. They saw the boycott as a threat to the way things had always been, and they were determined to stop it.

Laws were passed to make carpooling illegal, an

attempt to force people back onto the buses. Police officers targeted Black drivers who were giving rides to others, pulling them over and issuing tickets. Some were even arrested. The city put pressure on employers, threatening Black workers who were participating in the boycott. In some cases, people lost their jobs for simply choosing to walk instead of ride.

There was also violence. Homes of boycott leaders, including Dr. Martin Luther King Jr., were bombed. Churches that supported the movement were threatened. White mobs harassed Black walkers on the streets. The goal was to scare people into giving up the protest.

But it didn't work.

Instead of breaking apart, the movement grew stronger. The longer the boycott lasted, the more determined people became. The leadership of the Montgomery Improvement Association kept the community organized, ensuring that those who needed transportation could still get it. Walking became an act of resistance. Refusing to ride the bus was no longer just about getting to work—it was about demanding dignity and fairness.

The impact of the boycott spread beyond Montgomery. News of the protest reached other cities, and people across the country took notice. Black communities in other places began to discuss their own bus boycotts. The civil rights struggle that had often been ignored was now making headlines in newspapers nationwide.

As the months passed, the legal battle over segregation on buses continued. Civil rights lawyers argued that the laws forcing Black passengers to sit in the back were unconstitutional. They took the case to federal court, and after a long legal fight, the Supreme Court ruled that segregation on public buses was illegal. The decision was a major victory, not just for Montgomery, but for the entire Civil Rights Movement.

When the boycott finally ended, Black passengers returned to the buses—but this time, they could sit wherever they wanted. The rules that had controlled Montgomery's buses for so long had been struck down.

5

STANDING UP FOR CIVIL RIGHTS

After the boycott, life in Montgomery became difficult for her and her family. Many people saw her as a hero, but others saw her as a troublemaker. She lost her job as a seamstress, and her husband, Raymond, also lost his job. The threats against them did not stop, and finding work became nearly impossible. It was clear that staying in Montgomery was no longer safe, so they made the difficult decision to leave Alabama.

They moved to Detroit, Michigan, where Rosa Parks continued her activism. Some people assumed that once she was out of the South, life would be easier, but she quickly learned that racism and discrimination existed everywhere. Segregation was not the law in Detroit the way it had been in Montgomery, but Black residents still faced housing discrimination, police violence, and barriers to good jobs. Rosa Parks refused to ignore these issues.

She got involved in local civil rights work, joining protests and helping to support the growing movement against racial injustice. She worked with activists who were pushing for fair housing laws and equal job opportunities. She also helped expose police brutality in the city, standing with families who had lost loved ones to violence.

In the 1960s, the Civil Rights Movement was growing across the country, and Rosa Parks remained deeply involved. She attended marches, rallies, and protests, supporting leaders like Martin Luther King Jr. as they pushed for voting rights, school integration, and economic justice. She traveled to events, met with activists, and helped plan demonstrations that challenged unfair laws.

One of the most important events she attended was the 1963 March on Washington. More than 250,000 people gathered in the nation's capital to demand civil rights legislation. It was at this march that Martin Luther King Jr. gave his famous "I Have a Dream" speech. Rosa Parks was there, not as a speaker, but as a quiet, steady presence in the movement—someone who had already made history but continued to support the fight.

In 1965, the Voting Rights Act was signed into law, making it illegal to block Black Americans from voting. This was another major victory, but Rosa Parks knew that legal victories didn't always mean immediate change. She continued to work to ensure that Black citizens could safely register to vote, especially in the South, where intimidation was still common.

She also became an assistant to Congressman John Conyers, who was a strong supporter of civil rights in Detroit. She helped his office connect with the community, advocating for laws that would improve housing, education, and workers' rights. She used her experience to fight for those who were still struggling, making sure that their voices were heard in government.

Despite all of her efforts, life was not always easy. She and her husband continued to struggle financially, and for many years, they had little money. Even though she was widely respected, she did not receive the kind of support that many assumed she did. She never used her fame to gain personal wealth, instead dedicating her life to activism.

Later in life, she worked to inspire young people

to take part in the movement. She visited schools and spoke to students about the importance of standing up for what is right. She encouraged them to learn about history and to stay involved in their communities. She believed that the next generation had the power to continue the fight for justice.

Even as she got older, she remained active in the struggle for equality. She fought against apartheid in South Africa, a system of racial segregation that lasted until the early 1990s. She also spoke out against injustice in the United States, reminding people that racism had not disappeared just because laws had changed.

Working for the NAACP

Long before Rosa Parks became famous for refusing to give up her seat on a bus, she was already working for change. She believed that injustice had to be fought in every part of life—not just in public transportation but in schools, workplaces, and voting booths. One of the ways she did this was through her involvement with the National Association for the Advancement of Colored People (NAACP), an organization dedicated to fighting for civil rights.

Her work with the NAACP began in the early

1940s in Montgomery, Alabama. At the time, segregation was everywhere, and discrimination was not just legal—it was expected. Laws made it difficult for Black people to vote, get fair-paying jobs, or receive justice in the courts. The NAACP was one of the few organizations actively working to challenge these injustices. Rosa Parks knew this was the kind of work she wanted to be part of.

She started as a secretary for the Montgomery chapter of the NAACP. The job was not easy. The office received complaints from Black citizens who had been mistreated, arrested unfairly, or denied their rights. Rosa Parks helped record these cases, keeping track of what was happening and gathering evidence. She also wrote letters to officials, demanding justice for those who had been wronged.

One of her most important tasks was documenting cases of racial violence. In Alabama, Black people who were attacked, harassed, or even murdered often never saw justice. Police did little to investigate crimes committed against them, and all-white juries rarely convicted white attackers. The NAACP worked to bring attention to these cases, and Rosa Parks was deeply involved in collecting and organizing the details.

One case that had a deep impact on her was that

of Recy Taylor, a Black woman who was kidnapped and assaulted by a group of white men in 1944. Rosa Parks worked to bring attention to Taylor's case, organizing meetings and demanding action. Despite their efforts, the men responsible were never punished. Cases like this made it clear how deeply unfair the legal system was.

Her work also included helping Black citizens register to vote. Even though Black men and women had the legal right to vote, states like Alabama made it almost impossible for them to do so. They had to pass difficult literacy tests, pay poll taxes, and sometimes face threats if they even tried to register. Rosa Parks helped people prepare for the tests and encouraged them not to be afraid.

While working with the NAACP, she met many other activists who were fighting for civil rights. One of them was E.D. Nixon, a strong leader who believed that segregation could be defeated if people stood together. He played a major role in helping organize the Montgomery Bus Boycott after Rosa Parks' arrest. Their shared work in the NAACP helped build the foundation for that historic moment.

Even after the boycott, Rosa Parks' work did not stop. After moving to Detroit, she continued her involvement with civil rights organizations. She worked with the Southern Christian Leadership Conference (SCLC), an organization founded by Dr. Martin Luther King Jr. to promote nonviolent protests for equality. She also helped with voter registration efforts, making sure Black citizens had a voice in elections.

Speaking out for justice and equality

Rosa Parks was not someone who spoke loudly just to be heard. She was not the type of person who sought attention or wanted to be in the spotlight. But when it came to fighting for justice and equality, she understood that staying silent was not an option. She had spent years working behind the scenes, organizing, documenting injustices, and helping others find their voice. But after the Montgomery Bus Boycott, her role changed. People across the country wanted to hear from her. They wanted to understand why she had refused to move on the bus, what it meant for civil rights, and what could be done next.

She did not see herself as a natural public speaker, but she knew that words had power. Her quiet strength and steady determination inspired others. When she spoke, she didn't try to be dramatic or flashy. She told the truth. She described what it was like to live under segregation, how unfair laws made daily life difficult for Black Americans, and why change was necessary. She spoke about dignity, the right to be treated as an equal, and the importance of standing up against injustice.

One of the first times she spoke publicly after the boycott was during a fundraising event for the movement. The boycott had lasted over a year, and it had taken a toll on many people. Money was needed to continue legal battles and to support those who had lost their jobs for participating. Rosa Parks was asked to share her experience, and even though public speaking was not something she had done before, she agreed. She stood before the audience and described, in simple but powerful words, why she had refused to give up her seat and why the fight for civil rights could not stop with the buses.

Over time, speaking out became a larger part of her activism. She traveled to different cities to talk about what had happened in Montgomery and why it mattered everywhere. She met with students, community leaders, and church groups, encouraging them to get involved in the fight for equality. She reminded them that standing up against discrimination wasn't just about one moment—it was about changing an entire system.

She was invited to major civil rights events, including the 1963 March on Washington. While she did not give a speech there, her presence was important. She was part of the movement that had helped make that moment possible. She stood alongside leaders like Martin Luther King Jr. and John Lewis as they called for voting rights, equal education, and fair treatment under the law.

Even though she became well-known, she never used her fame for personal gain. She remained focused on the work, continuing to support civil rights organizations and speaking whenever she could about the injustices that still needed to be fought. She knew that just because the buses had been desegregated, that did not mean equality had been achieved. Schools, jobs, and housing were still deeply unequal. Laws had changed, but discrimination still shaped daily life for many Black Americans.

How her courage inspired new laws

The success of the boycott showed that nonviolent protest could make a difference. It inspired other civil rights activists to take action in their own cities. Across the South, sit-ins, marches, and boycotts were organized to challenge segregation in restaurants, schools, and businesses. Rosa Parks' quiet act of resistance had helped prove that ordinary people could stand up against unfair laws—and win.

Her courage also helped pave the way for the Civil Rights Act of 1964. This law made segregation illegal in public places, including restaurants, hotels, and schools. It also banned discrimination based on race, color, religion, sex, or national origin. For decades, Black Americans had been forced to use separate restrooms, drink from different water fountains, and attend underfunded schools. This law made those practices illegal.

Another important law that was influenced by the civil rights movement was the Voting Rights Act of 1965. Even though Black Americans technically had the right to vote, many Southern states made it almost impossible for them to do so. They were forced to take difficult literacy tests, pay unfair taxes, or face threats and violence just for trying to register. The Voting Rights Act banned these practices, making it easier for Black citizens to have a voice in elections.

Rosa Parks continued to fight for justice long

after these laws were passed. She knew that changing laws was important, but changing people's attitudes was just as necessary. Even after segregation was officially outlawed, many Black Americans still faced discrimination in housing, education, and employment. She spent much of her life working to make sure the rights that had been won were actually put into practice.

Her influence extended beyond the United States. Her story became known around the world, inspiring other movements for justice. People fighting against unfair governments in other countries looked to her as proof that one person's actions could make a difference. She showed that courage was not just about grand speeches or political power —it was about standing firm in the face of injustice, even when it was difficult.

6

ROSA PARKS' LATER YEARS

In 1957, Rosa Parks and her family made the difficult decision to leave Montgomery and move to Detroit, Michigan. Detroit was known as the "Motor City" because of its automobile industry, and many Black families had moved there for better opportunities. It was part of what was known as the Great Migration—a time when millions of Black Americans left the South to escape segregation and find better jobs in the North. Rosa and Raymond hoped that life in Detroit would be different.

Segregation was not written into law in Detroit the way it had been in Alabama, but discrimination was still everywhere. Black families struggled to find good housing because many landlords refused to rent to them. Schools in Black neighborhoods received fewer resources than those in white neighborhoods. Many jobs paid Black workers less than white workers, even if they had the same skills and experience. Racism was not just a Southern problem —it existed all over the country.

Rosa Parks did not sit back and accept these injustices. She had spent years fighting for equality in Montgomery, and she was not going to stop just because she had moved to a new city. In Detroit, she became involved in new battles for civil rights.

One of her first major roles was working for Congressman John Conyers. He was a strong supporter of civil rights and believed in making real changes in laws to help Black Americans. Rosa Parks worked as his secretary and helped him connect with people in the community. She used her position to advocate for fair housing, voting rights, and equal job opportunities. She also helped struggling families, meeting with people who had been mistreated and finding ways to help them.

Housing discrimination was one of the biggest problems in Detroit. Black families were often forced to live in crowded, poorly maintained neighborhoods because landlords and banks made it difficult for them to rent or buy homes in white areas. Rosa Parks joined protests and worked with organizations that fought against these unfair housing policies. She knew that having a safe and decent place to live was just as important as being able to sit anywhere on a bus.

She also spoke out against police brutality. Many Black residents in Detroit were targeted by unfair and sometimes violent treatment from police officers. There were cases where unarmed Black men were beaten or even killed by police, and nothing was done about it. Rosa Parks refused to stay silent. She worked with civil rights groups to demand justice for victims of police violence.

Honored with awards

Rosa Parks never set out to be famous. She didn't take a stand on that Montgomery bus because she wanted recognition. She did it because she knew the rules were unfair, and she was tired of seeing Black people treated as less than equal. But as the years went on, people across the country—and the world—came to understand just how important her actions had been.

By the time Rosa Parks was in her later years, she had become a symbol of courage and justice. She was invited to speak at schools, colleges, and events where people wanted to learn from her example. She continued working for civil rights, never stopping in her fight for equality. Even though she was not someone who looked for praise, people knew that what she had done deserved to be recognized.

Over the years, she received many awards and honors. She was given keys to cities, honorary degrees from universities, and statues were built in her honor. But two of the most important awards she received were the **Presidential Medal of Freedom** and the **Congressional Gold Medal**, two of the highest honors that a person in the United States can receive.

In 1996, President Bill Clinton awarded Rosa Parks the Presidential Medal of Freedom. This award is given to people who have made a great impact on the country, whether in the arts, science, politics, or human rights. When she was given the medal, President Clinton spoke about how her bravery had changed the course of history. He recognized that her decision to stay seated on that bus in 1955 had set off a movement that led to greater justice for all Americans.

Even as she stood in front of the cameras receiving one of the highest honors in the nation, Rosa Parks remained humble. She did not see herself as someone who deserved special recognition. She often said that she was just one person who had done what she knew was right. But the truth was that her quiet strength had led to some of the biggest changes in American history.

A few years later, in 1999, she was awarded the Congressional Gold Medal. This is one of the highest honors that Congress can give, and it is awarded to people who have made a lasting impact on the country. It is rare for someone to receive both the Presidential Medal of Freedom and the Congressional Gold Medal, but Rosa Parks was one of the few people in history to be given both.

How Rosa Parks became a symbol of resistance

Rosa Parks had never set out to be famous. She had never planned to become a symbol of resistance. When she refused to give up her seat on that Montgomery bus in 1955, she was simply standing up for her rights, just as she had always done in small ways throughout her life. But the impact of her decision spread far beyond that moment, and by the time she reached her later years, she had become one of the most recognized figures in the fight for justice.

Her name was spoken in classrooms, written in history books, and honored by leaders all over the world. People saw her as proof that one person's courage could make a difference. For many, she represented the power of quiet strength—the idea that you don't have to be loud or famous to create change.

Her influence wasn't limited to the United States. Around the world, people fighting against injustice in their own countries looked to her as an example. Leaders in movements against unfair governments, discrimination, and inequality pointed to Rosa Parks as proof that standing firm in the face of oppression could lead to real change. She had inspired the Civil

Rights Movement in America, but her story was universal.

Even as she aged, Rosa Parks continued to be a voice for justice. She was invited to speak at events where activists gathered to discuss ways to fight inequality. She met with young people who wanted to learn from her experiences. She encouraged them to be strong in their beliefs and to never accept unfair treatment as something normal.

She also became a symbol of endurance. She had faced threats, lost jobs, and struggled financially because of her role in the civil rights movement. But she had never backed down. She had never stopped believing in equality. Even in difficult times, she had continued to push forward.

Her image became iconic. Pictures of her on the bus, standing next to Martin Luther King Jr., and receiving awards were shared in schools and museums. She became a face of resistance—a reminder of what could happen when someone chose to stand up, or in her case, stay seated.

Her influence extended beyond activists and history books. Artists created paintings and sculptures of her. Musicians wrote songs about her courage. Movies and documentaries were made about her life. The more time passed, the more people realized that Rosa Parks was not just part of history—she was part of the present and the future, too.

7

ROSA PARKS' LEGACY

Rosa Parks changed history with one simple act of defiance, and the impact of her courage is still felt today. Long after her passing, people continue to honor her life, her bravery, and the movement she helped shape. Her name is known around the world, and she is remembered not just as a woman who refused to give up her seat, but as someone who stood up against injustice in all its forms.

In cities across the United States, streets, schools, and public buildings bear her name. There is Rosa Parks Boulevard in Detroit, Rosa Parks Elementary Schools in different states, and even parks and libraries dedicated to her memory. These places serve as daily reminders of what she stood for—fairness, dignity, and equality for all people.

In Washington, D.C., a statue of Rosa Parks stands in the United States Capitol. It was placed there in 2013, making her the first Black woman to have a full-length statue in the Capitol building. The statue captures her strength, showing her seated with a determined expression, just as she had been on that historic day in Montgomery. People from all over the world visit the Capitol and see her statue, learning about her impact on American history.

Her story is also told in museums and exhibits. The National Civil Rights Museum in Memphis, Tennessee, features an entire section dedicated to Rosa Parks and the Montgomery Bus Boycott. Visitors can step inside a replica of the bus where she took her stand, seeing firsthand the setting of that historic moment. Her preserved belongings, letters, and documents are displayed in museums, helping people understand the struggles she faced and the work she did beyond that one day on the bus.

Each year on December 1, the anniversary of the day she was arrested, schools and communities hold events to celebrate her life and legacy. Students learn about her courage and the power of standing up for what is right. Some schools hold essay contests where children write about what Rosa Parks means to them. Others have reenactments of the Montgomery Bus Boycott to help students understand the sacrifices people made to end segregation.

The impact of her actions

Rosa Parks' decision to stay seated on a bus in Montgomery, Alabama, didn't just change her own life—it changed the future. Her actions sent a message that one person could make a difference, and that message has been passed down to every generation since. The impact of what she did reaches far beyond the Civil Rights Movement of the 1950s and 1960s. It continues to inspire young people today to stand up for fairness, speak out against injustice, and believe that change is possible.

HER STORY HAS BECOME a lesson in courage for students all over the world. In classrooms, children learn about how one woman's quiet strength helped launch a movement that changed the laws of the United States. Teachers use her example to show that doing what is right is not always easy, but it is always important. Students are encouraged to think about ways they can stand up for what they believe in, whether in their schools, communities, or beyond.

Her impact is seen in the way young activists continue to fight for justice today. Whether they are speaking out against discrimination, organizing protests, or working to change unfair laws, they often point to Rosa Parks as one of their inspirations. Her bravery showed that change doesn't always come from people in positions of power—it often comes from ordinary people who refuse to accept what is wrong.

Many leaders in movements for equal rights have spoken about how Rosa Parks influenced them. Some have fought for racial justice, while others have worked for gender equality, disability rights, and fair treatment for all people. They have drawn strength from her example, knowing that standing up for what is right can be difficult, but it is necessary.

. . .

HER INFLUENCE CAN ALSO BE SEEN in the arts, where writers, musicians, and filmmakers have told her story in books, songs, and movies. These works help keep her legacy alive, making sure that new generations continue to learn about her courage and its lasting impact.

Lessons kids can learn from her courage and determination

One of the biggest lessons kids can learn from Rosa Parks is that one person can make a difference. When she refused to give up her seat, she wasn't trying to start a movement. She was simply standing up for herself. But that small act of resistance led to a huge change. It proves that even small decisions can have a big impact. When kids see something unfair, they should know that speaking up, even in a small way, can be the first step toward change.

ANOTHER LESSON IS about standing up for what is right, even when it's hard. It wasn't easy for Rosa Parks to say no to the bus driver. She knew the rules of segregation, and she knew what could happen if she didn't follow them. But she also knew the rules were wrong. It takes courage to speak out against unfair treatment, especially when others around you are staying silent. Kids can learn from her that doing the right thing is not always easy, but it is always important.

HER STORY also teaches the importance of staying strong in the face of challenges. After she was arrested, life didn't suddenly get better. She lost her job, she and her husband faced threats, and they had to leave Montgomery. But she didn't stop fighting for civil rights. Even after she moved to Detroit, she kept working to make things better for others. Life will always have challenges, but Rosa Parks showed that staying strong and not giving up is the key to making a difference.

ANOTHER LESSON from her life is that change takes time and teamwork. Rosa Parks didn't end segregation on her own. Her refusal to move sparked the Montgomery Bus Boycott, but thousands of people had to work together to make it successful. She understood that big changes don't happen overnight. They take time, effort, and people working together.

Kids can learn that when they want to make a difference, they don't have to do it alone. By working with others who share their goals, they can create real change.

Her story is also a reminder that respect and kindness are powerful. Rosa Parks never responded with anger or violence, even when people were unfair to her. She believed in peaceful resistance and treating people with dignity. Kids can learn that being kind and respectful, even in tough situations, can be one of the strongest ways to stand up for what is right.

Another important lesson is about believing in yourself. Before she made history, Rosa Parks was just a regular person who worked hard and cared about her community. She didn't have special powers or a big title—she was simply a woman who knew that unfair rules needed to change. Her story teaches kids that they don't have to be famous or powerful to make a difference. They just need to believe in themselves and be willing to take action when they see something wrong.

CONCLUSION

Rosa Parks' life was dedicated to fairness, justice, and the belief that everyone should be treated with dignity. She is often remembered for one powerful moment—the day she refused to give up her seat on a Montgomery bus. But her impact stretched far beyond that day. Her actions helped inspire a movement, changed unfair laws, and encouraged generations of people to stand up for what is right.

Her courage on December 1, 1955, was the spark that ignited the Montgomery Bus Boycott, a movement that lasted over a year and proved that ordinary people could demand change through peaceful protest. She was not the first person to challenge segregation on public transportation, but she became the face of the movement because of her quiet strength and determination. Her arrest did not scare her into silence—it pushed her to continue the fight.

She was more than a symbol; she was an activist who worked for change long before and long after the bus boycott. As a secretary for the NAACP, she helped document cases of racial injustice, giving a voice to people who had been ignored. Her efforts in voter registration and civil rights activism showed that she was committed to making sure Black Americans had the same opportunities and rights as everyone else.

Moving to Detroit did not end her fight. She worked for fair housing, equal job opportunities, and justice for people who had been treated unfairly by the legal system. She knew that discrimination was not just a problem in the South—it was something that needed to be addressed everywhere. She spent decades speaking out against racism and injustice, standing alongside other leaders in the Civil Rights Movement.

Her commitment to fairness earned her some of the highest honors in the United States, including the Presidential Medal of Freedom and the Congressional Gold Medal. These awards recognized the impact of her lifelong work, but they were not what motivated her. She never stood up for recognition—she stood up because it was the right thing to do.

Rosa Parks' influence did not end with the Civil Rights Movement. Her story continues to inspire young people to believe that their voices matter. Schools, streets, and museums carry her name, not just to honor her, but to remind people of what she stood for.

Her life is proof that one person's actions can make a difference. She showed that bravery isn't about being the loudest or the strongest—it's about standing firm in the face of injustice. Her determination helped change laws, but more importantly, it changed the way people think about fairness, equality, and the power of standing up for what is right.

Her legacy is not just about what she did in the past. It is about what people continue to do because of her example. Her courage, strength, and commitment to justice serve as a reminder that everyone has the power to create change, no matter their age, background, or circumstances.

Why one person's bravery can make a difference

Rosa Parks showed the world that courage is not about being the loudest or the strongest. It is about standing firm in what is right, even when others tell you to sit down. Her bravery on that Montgomery bus was not an accident. It was the result of years of seeing injustice and deciding that enough was enough. She knew the risk, but she also knew that nothing would change if people stayed silent.

One person's actions can inspire thousands, even millions. Rosa Parks was just one woman, but her decision led to the Montgomery Bus Boycott, which forced the country to confront the unfair laws of segregation. Her bravery helped push the Civil Rights Movement forward, showing that everyday people had the power to demand change. If she had given up her seat, history might have unfolded very differently.

Bravery does not always look the same. Some people show courage by speaking up when they see something wrong. Others stand up for their rights even when they are afraid. Some work quietly behind the scenes to help others. The important thing is that bravery is not limited to a few special people—it is something anyone can have.

The choices people make every day can shape the future. If someone sees another person being treated unfairly, they have a choice: ignore it or speak up. If a rule is unfair, they can either accept it or challenge it. Rosa Parks did not have power, money, or a big platform when she made her stand. She was a regular person who made a decision that changed history. That means anyone can do the same.

Standing up for what is right is not always easy. It can be scary to challenge unfairness, especially when it feels like no one else is willing to. But history has shown that real change happens when even one person refuses to accept what is wrong. When others see that kind of courage, they feel braver too.

Rosa Parks did not act alone, but her courage helped inspire the people around her to take action. The bus boycott succeeded because thousands of others joined in, walking instead of riding. But it all started with her one decision. That is how movements begin—one person at a time.

Her story is a reminder that bravery is not about being fearless. It is about doing what is right even when fear is present. Every person has the ability to make a difference, whether it is by standing up for a friend, challenging an unfair rule, or working toward a better future.

Change does not happen overnight. It takes time, persistence, and people who are willing to do what is right, even when it is hard. Rosa Parks knew this. She continued fighting for justice long after her famous moment on the bus. Her life showed that bravery is not just a single act—it is a way of living.

Her legacy is a challenge to every generation. It asks people to think about the kind of world they want to live in and what they are willing to do to make it better. One person's bravery can set off a chain reaction, and history proves that ordinary people can change the world.

GLOSSARY
SEGREGATION

Segregation means keeping people apart because of their race, religion, or background. In the United States, segregation was a system that forced Black and white people to use separate schools, restaurants, buses, and even drinking fountains. The rules were designed to make Black Americans feel like second-class citizens. Signs were put up to remind people where they could or couldn't go. Even though segregation was unfair, it was the law in many places for a long time. People like Rosa Parks helped fight against it so that everyone could be treated equally.

Boycott

A boycott happens when people refuse to buy, use, or support something to protest unfair treatment. The Montgomery Bus Boycott is one of the most famous examples. When Rosa Parks was arrested for not giving up her seat, Black residents of Montgomery stopped riding the buses. They wanted to show that they would not support a system that treated them unfairly. The boycott lasted for over a year, and without Black riders, the bus system lost a lot of money. In the end, the Supreme Court ruled that bus segregation was illegal. The boycott proved that when people work together, they can create change.

Civil Rights

Civil rights are the basic freedoms and protections that every person should have, no matter their race, gender, or background. These rights include the right to vote, the right to go to school, and the right to be treated fairly. The Civil Rights Movement was a fight to make sure these rights were given to all people, not just some. Rosa Parks, Dr. Martin Luther King Jr., and many others worked to end laws that discriminated against Black Americans and denied them their rights.

Jim Crow Laws

Jim Crow laws were rules that enforced segregation in the South. They kept Black and white people separate in public places and allowed businesses, schools, and even hospitals to refuse service to Black

Americans. These laws made life unfair for Black people by giving them fewer opportunities for jobs, education, and housing. The Civil Rights Movement fought to get rid of these laws so that everyone could be treated equally.

Nonviolent Protest

Nonviolent protest is a way of standing up against unfair laws and treatment without using violence. Instead of fighting, people use marches, sit-ins, boycotts, and peaceful demonstrations to demand change. Rosa Parks' refusal to move on the bus was a form of nonviolent protest. Dr. Martin Luther King Jr. also encouraged peaceful protests as a way to fight for civil rights. These methods showed that people could stand up for justice without hurting others.

Activist

An activist is someone who works to make the world a better place by standing up for what is right. Activists fight against unfair laws, speak out for people who are being mistreated, and work to change things for the better. Rosa Parks was an activist because she didn't just accept unfair rules—she challenged them. Many other people joined her in the fight for civil rights, proving that activism is often stronger when people work together.

Discrimination

Discrimination happens when people are treated unfairly just because of who they are. This can be based on race, gender, religion, or other factors. In Rosa Parks' time, Black Americans faced discrimination in many ways, from being denied good jobs to being forced to attend underfunded schools. The Civil Rights Movement worked to stop discrimination and create a society where everyone has the same opportunities.

Supreme Court

The Supreme Court is the highest court in the United States. It has the power to decide if laws are fair or unfair. Many important decisions about civil rights were made by the Supreme Court, including the ruling that segregation on buses was illegal. When the court makes a decision, all states must follow it.

Equality

Equality means that everyone is treated fairly and has the same rights. The Civil Rights Movement fought for equality so that Black Americans could have the same opportunities as white Americans. Rosa Parks believed that no one should be treated as less important just because of their race. She spent her life working to make sure all people were treated with respect.

Integration

Integration is the opposite of segregation. It means bringing people of all races and backgrounds together, instead of keeping them separate. After the Montgomery Bus Boycott and other protests, buses, schools, and businesses were integrated. This allowed people to sit where they wanted, attend the same schools, and have equal opportunities in their communities.

March on Washington

The March on Washington was one of the biggest civil rights events in history. In 1963, more than 250,000 people gathered in Washington, D.C., to demand justice and equality. Dr. Martin Luther King Jr. gave his famous "I Have a Dream" speech at this event. Rosa Parks attended the march, showing her continued dedication to the movement. The march helped lead to new laws that protected civil rights.

Voting Rights Act

The Voting Rights Act of 1965 was a law that made it illegal to stop people from voting based on their race. Before this law, many Black Americans were prevented from voting through unfair tests, high taxes, and threats. The Civil Rights Movement worked hard to make sure everyone had the right to vote, and Rosa Parks supported these efforts. This law helped bring more fairness to elections and gave Black Americans a stronger voice in government.

Congressional Gold Medal

The Congressional Gold Medal is one of the highest honors a person can receive in the United States. Rosa Parks was awarded this medal in 1999 for her lifelong dedication to justice and equality. It was a way of recognizing that her actions had changed history and inspired millions of people.

Presidential Medal of Freedom

The Presidential Medal of Freedom is another great honor, given to people who have made a major impact on the country. Rosa Parks received this medal in 1996 from President Bill Clinton. It was a way of thanking her for standing up for justice and showing that one person's courage can change the world.

FUN FACTS

She Wasn't the First to Refuse to Give Up Her Seat

Long before Rosa Parks made history in 1955, other Black Americans had challenged segregation on public transportation. Claudette Colvin, a 15-year-old girl, refused to give up her seat on a Montgomery bus nine months before Rosa Parks' arrest. There were also cases in other states where people had stood up against unfair bus rules. What made Rosa Parks' case different was the way it sparked a movement. Civil rights leaders knew she was a respected member of the community, and they believed her case could rally people together to demand change.

She Had a Strong Sense of Justice from a Young Age

As a child, Rosa Parks was bothered by the way Black people were treated unfairly. She once saw a white boy threaten to hit her, and instead of backing away, she stood her ground. Her grandmother warned her to stay out of trouble, but Rosa Parks didn't think it was fair that Black children were expected to accept mistreatment. That sense of injustice stayed with her throughout her life.

She Was an Investigator for the NAACP

Before she became famous for her bus protest, Rosa Parks was already working to fight discrimination. As the secretary for the Montgomery chapter of the NAACP, she helped document cases where Black people were treated unfairly. One of her biggest roles was investigating cases of violence against Black women. She worked to bring attention to their stories and demand justice.

She Was Arrested More Than Once

Most people know about her arrest on the bus in 1955, but Rosa Parks was arrested again in 1956 during the Montgomery Bus Boycott. She and others were taken into custody for organizing the protest against segregation. She knew that standing up for civil rights could be risky, but she didn't let that stop her from fighting for justice.

She Moved to Detroit and Continued Fighting for Civil Rights

After the boycott, Rosa Parks and her husband faced serious threats and struggled to find work in Montgomery. In 1957, they moved to Detroit, Michigan, hoping for a fresh start. Even though segregation was not legal in Detroit the way it was in the South, discrimination still existed. She continued her activism there, working on issues like housing discrimination, fair pay, and police brutality.

She Worked for a U.S. Congressman

Many years after her famous protest, Rosa Parks worked for Congressman John Conyers. She helped connect him with the community and made sure that people's concerns were heard. She never wanted to stop fighting for equality, and she believed that government leaders should listen to the voices of everyday people.

She Received the Presidential Medal of Freedom

In 1996, Rosa Parks was awarded the Presidential Medal of Freedom, one of the highest honors a U.S. citizen can receive. It was given to her by President Bill Clinton as a way to recognize her lifelong fight for justice and equality.

She Also Received the Congressional Gold Medal

In 1999, Rosa Parks received another top honor, the Congressional Gold Medal. It was awarded to her in Washington, D.C., in front of lawmakers who wanted to recognize how much she had done to change the country. Few people receive both the Presidential Medal of Freedom and the Congressional Gold Medal, but Rosa Parks' impact on history was too important to ignore.

A Bus Seat Was Left Empty in Her Honor

After she passed away in 2005, cities across the country paid tribute to her. Some public buses kept a front seat empty with a sign honoring her memory. It was a powerful way to show how one act of defiance could change history.

She Was the First Woman to Lie in Honor at the U.S. Capitol

When Rosa Parks passed away, she was given an honor usually reserved for presidents and important government leaders. Her body was placed in the U.S. Capitol so people could visit and pay their respects. She was the first woman in American history to receive this tribute. Thousands of people came to honor her life and the impact she had made.

DISCUSSION QUESTIONS

Why do you think Rosa Parks refused to give up her seat?

Rosa Parks had seen unfair treatment her entire life. She knew the bus rules were unjust, and she had reached a point where she didn't want to accept them anymore. Her decision was about more than just one seat—it was about standing up for fairness. What would you have done in her situation? Do you think it would have been difficult to stay seated when the bus driver told her to move?

What do you think it felt like to be Rosa Parks that day?

Getting arrested is a scary experience. Rosa Parks knew there would be consequences for refusing to move, but she stayed calm and did not back down.

Do you think she was nervous? How do you think she found the courage to stand up for herself?

How did her actions affect other people?

Her arrest led to the Montgomery Bus Boycott, which lasted for more than a year. People walked miles instead of taking the bus, showing that they were willing to sacrifice for what they believed in. Do you think Rosa Parks knew that her decision would lead to something so big? What does this say about how one person can inspire many others?

Why do you think the Montgomery Bus Boycott worked?

The boycott was successful because so many people came together and refused to use the buses. Black riders made up most of the bus system's customers, so without them, the bus companies lost money. Do you think the boycott would have worked if only a few people participated? What does this teach about working together for change?

What would have happened if Rosa Parks had moved to another seat instead of refusing?

If Rosa Parks had followed the rules that day, history might have taken a different path. The Civil Rights Movement may have moved forward in another way, but her choice helped bring attention to the problem of segregation. Why do you think her act of defiance became such a powerful moment in history?

How do you think life would be different today if Rosa Parks and other activists had not fought against segregation?

Laws changed because of the Civil Rights Movement, but what if they hadn't? Schools, restaurants, and buses could still be segregated. People of color might not have the same rights and opportunities. How do the actions of people in the past shape the world today?

What lessons can be learned from Rosa Parks' story?

Her story is about bravery, standing up for fairness, and never giving up. She didn't have special powers or a big platform—she was just one person who made a choice. What are some ways that people today can follow her example? How can kids stand up for what's right in their schools and communities?

How do people today honor Rosa Parks' legacy?

Many schools, streets, and buildings are named after Rosa Parks. She has statues, her bus is displayed in museums, and she received some of the highest honors in the country. Why do you think people continue to honor her today? What does it say about the lasting impact of her actions?

Do you think standing up for what is right is always easy?

Rosa Parks lost her job after her arrest. She and her husband faced threats, and life became more difficult for them. Speaking out for justice is not always easy, but she did not regret her decision. What do you think gave her the strength to keep fighting for civil rights?

How can kids today help make the world a better place?

Rosa Parks saw something unfair and took action. Kids today may not face the same struggles, but there are still ways to make a difference. What are some things that kids can do in their schools and communities to make sure people are treated fairly? How can small acts of kindness and fairness lead to bigger change?